Tadpoles to
Frogs

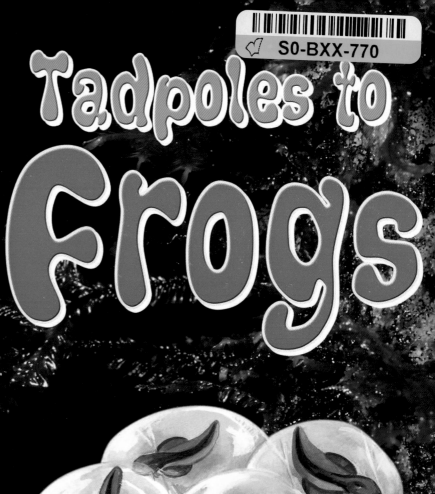

Bobbie Kalman

Crabtree Publishing Company

www.crabtreebooks.com

It's fun to learn about Baby Animals

Created by Bobbie Kalman

Dedicated by Margaret Amy Salter
To my beautiful son Aiden—you are my world
and my everything.

**Author and
Editor-in-Chief**
Bobbie Kalman

Editor
Kathy Middleton

Proofreader
Crystal Sikkens

Photo research
Bobbie Kalman
Crystal Sikkens

Design
Bobbie Kalman
Katherine Berti
Samantha Crabtree
     (logo and front cover)

Production coordinator
Katherine Berti

Illustrations
Katherine Berti: pages 6, 8 (left),
     24 (skeleton and lungs)
Bonna Rouse: pages 1, 8 (right),
     12, 16, 24 (legs and life cycle)

Photographs
© BigStockPhoto.com: pages 4 (bottom), 10 (frogs with eggs),
     11 (bottom), 24 (eggs)
© Dreamstime.com: pages 9 (bottom), 16 (middle)
© iStockphoto.com: front cover (tadpole), pages 5 (top right),
     10 (inset), 14 (top), 15 (top), 16 (bottom), 21 (middle right
     and bottom right), 22 (left), 24 (gills and tadpole)
© Justin Touchon: page 12
© robertmccaw.com: page 17 (top)
© Shutterstock.com: covers (except tadpole), pages 1, 3, 4 (top),
     5 (bottom), 6, 7, 8, 9 (top), 10 (background), 11 (top and
     background), 13, 14 (bottom), 15 (bottom), 17 (bottom), 18,
     19, 20, 21 (top, middle left, and bottom left), 22 (right), 23,
     24 (adults, froglets, skin, and tree frog)

Library and Archives Canada Cataloguing in Publication

Kalman, Bobbie, 1947-
     Tadpoles to frogs / Bobbie Kalman.

(It's fun to learn about baby animals)
Includes index.
ISBN 978-0-7787-3956-2 (bound).--ISBN 978-0-7787-3975-3 (pbk.)

     1. Tadpoles--Juvenile literature. 2. Frogs--Development--Juvenile
literature. I. Title. II. Series.

QL668.E2K365 2008   j597.8'9139   C2008-907019-4

Library of Congress Cataloging-in-Publication Data

Kalman, Bobbie.
     Tadpoles to frogs / Bobbie Kalman.
         p. cm. -- (It's fun to learn about baby animals)
     Includes index.
     ISBN 978-0-7787-3975-3 (pbk. : alk. paper) -- ISBN 978-0-7787-3956-2
(reinforced library binding : alk. paper)
     1. Tadpoles--Juvenile literature. 2. Frogs--Life cycles--Juvenile literature. I.
Title. II. Series.

QL668.E2K346 2009
597.8'9139--dc22
                                        2008046252

Crabtree Publishing Company

Printed in Canada/042019/MQ20190301

www.crabtreebooks.com   1-800-387-7650

Published in Canada
Crabtree Publishing
616 Welland Ave.
St. Catharines, Ontario
L2M 5V6

Published in the United States
Crabtree Publishing
PMB 59051
350 Fifth Avenue, 59th Floor
New York, New York 10118

Published in the United Kingdom
Crabtree Publishing
Maritime House
Basin Road North, Hove
BN41 1WR

Published in Australia
Crabtree Publishing
Unit 3 – 5
Currumbin Court
Capalaba QLD 4157

What is in this book?

Fantastic frogs!

tomato frog

There are about 4,000 kinds of frogs. Frogs are animals called **amphibians**. The word "amphibian" means "two lives." Frogs have two parts to their lives. They live the first part of their lives in water.

adult frog

frog eggs

*Baby frogs start their lives as eggs. They change a lot before they become **adult** frogs. Adult frogs are fully grown. These eggs are in water. What will happen to them next?*

When frogs are fully grown, they live mainly on land. Some frogs live close to the ground. Other frogs live in trees. Frogs that live in trees are called tree frogs.

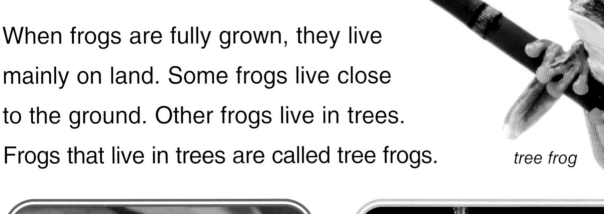

tree frog

This frog lives on land near a pond.
Frogs need water to keep their skin wet.

This Amazon leaf frog lives in trees.
Its body is made for climbing.

Bones, blood, and skin

Frogs are animals called **vertebrates**. Vertebrates have **backbones** and other bones inside their bodies. All their bones make up a **skeleton**.

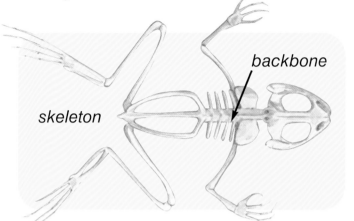

backbone

skeleton

Frogs are **cold-blooded**. They cannot warm or cool their bodies from the inside. They warm up in the sun. They cool off in water.

Slimy skin

A frog's skin is covered in **mucus**, or slime. Mucus keeps a frog's skin **moist**, or wet. Some frogs have skin that gives off **poison**. Poison protects frogs from **predators**. Predators are animals that hunt and eat other animals. Poison can make predators sick.

These frogs are poison dart frogs. Their skin gives off poison.

This bullfrog feels slimy in the girl's hands.

Frog bodies

Frogs breathe air above water. They take in air through their noses and breathe with **lungs**. Frogs also breathe through tiny **pores**, or holes, in their skin.

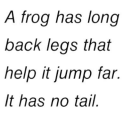

A frog has long back legs that help it jump far. It has no tail.

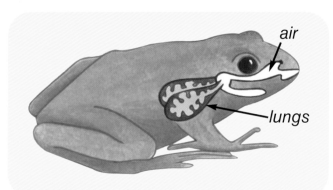

tree frog

Tree frogs have pads on their toes. The pads stick to plants as the frog climbs.

Frogs that spend a lot of time in water have webs between their toes.

web

sticky pads

Frog sense

Frogs have five senses. Their senses are sight, hearing, touch, smell, and taste. Frogs use their senses to find food and to get away from predators.

*Frogs have large round ears. The ears are covered by skin called a **tympanum**.*

A frog has big eyes at the top of its head. It can see in different directions at the same time.

tympanu

extra eyelid

Most frogs have an extra eyelid to protect their eyes under water and when they jump.

Big life changes

Frogs do not look like their parents when they are babies. They go through a big set of changes called **metamorphosis**. They change completely as they grow to become frogs.

clump of eggs

These frogs have laid their eggs in water. The eggs stick together in clumps like jelly.

Frogs start their lives inside eggs. Frog eggs are called **spawn**. The dark spots inside the eggs will become **tadpoles**.

spawn

tadpoles

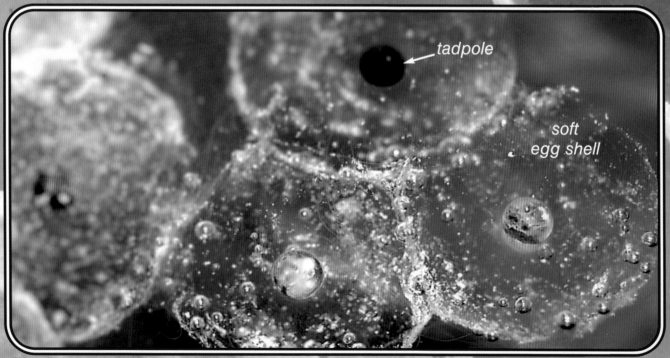

tadpole

soft egg shell

This picture shows the eggs close up. The dark spots are tadpoles. Around the tadpoles are egg shells, which are soft and clear, like jelly.

Tree frog eggs

tree frog tadpoles on a leaf

Tree frogs lay very few eggs. Some lay their eggs in small pools of water that they find on leaves. Other tree frogs carry their eggs around on their backs.

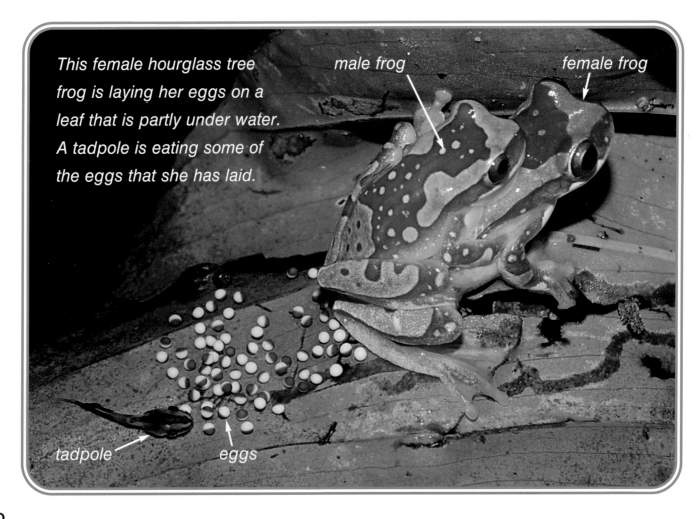

This female hourglass tree frog is laying her eggs on a leaf that is partly under water. A tadpole is eating some of the eggs that she has laid.

male frog

female frog

tadpole

eggs

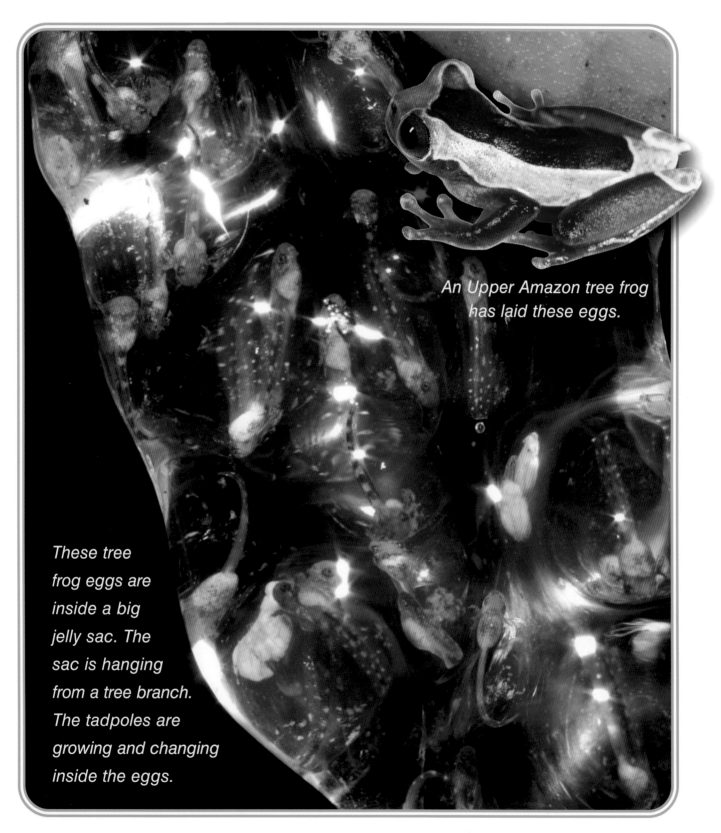

An Upper Amazon tree frog
has laid these eggs.

These tree
frog eggs are
inside a big
jelly sac. The
sac is hanging
from a tree branch.
The tadpoles are
growing and changing
inside the eggs.

Eggs to tadpoles

gills

One to three weeks later, a tadpole **hatches**, or breaks out of its egg. The tadpole has a head and a tail. It also has **gills** for breathing under water. You can see the gills in the picture on the left. Tadpoles cannot breathe above water. They breathe the way fish breathe.

Tadpoles that live in water hang on to plants when they first hatch.

This poison dart frog is carrying several tadpoles on its back.

Piggyback

Poison dart frogs carry their tadpoles on their backs. They then place each tadpole into a puddle of water on a leaf. The tadpoles keep growing in the puddles.

This poison dart frog is carrying one tadpole.

15

Growing legs

The tadpole grows bigger and longer. After about nine weeks, it starts to grow back legs. Its gills are gone. The tadpole now has lungs inside its body for breathing.

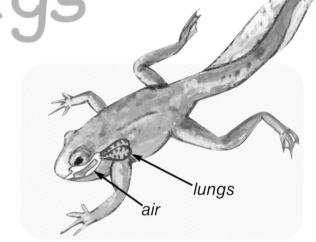

lungs

air

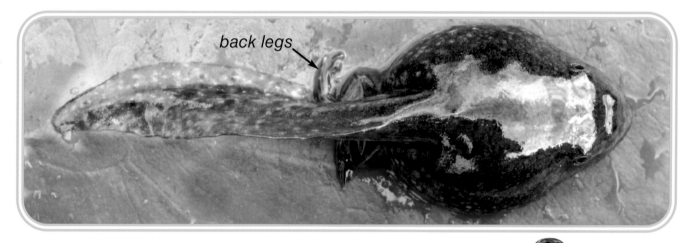

back legs

The front legs are where the gills used to be.

This tadpole lives in water and eats plants. It swims above water to breathe.

This tree frog tadpole lives on plants. It can breathe air now.

Losing their tails

At three to five months, a frog starts to lose its tail. The tail does not fall off. It becomes smaller and smaller until it is gone. The tadpole is now called a **froglet**. The froglet looks like its parents. It also starts to eat different food. The tadpole ate plants, but a frog eats insects and other small animals.

(left) This tree frog's tail is getting shorter. It will soon be gone.
The froglet now looks like a frog.

This young white-lined monkey frog has no tail, but it is still growing and changing.

Its colors will get darker when it becomes an adult.

White-lined monkey frogs are tree frogs. Their long toes have no webs.

A frog's life cycle

When frogs become adults, they are able to **mate**, or make babies. Frogs mate in ponds or even in puddles. Some frogs lay eggs only in the ponds where they hatched. These frogs go back to the same ponds to mate.

throat sac

Some male frogs puff out their throat sacs and make loud noises to tell female frogs that they want to mate.

A frog's life cycle

Female frogs lay eggs, and tadpoles hatch. A new **life cycle** starts. A life cycle is the set of changes that takes place from a frog egg to an adult frog.

A female frog lays eggs.

eggs

A tadpole hatches.

An adult frog can make babies.

It is now a froglet with a small tail.

The tadpole grows legs.

Are these frogs?

Which of these animals are frogs? Which are not frogs?

These animals look like frogs, but they are toads. The back legs of toads are shorter than the back legs of frogs. The skin of toads is drier and bumpier than the skin of frogs. The toads above and left are green toads. The toad below is a fire-bellied toad.

Is this a crown prince or a frog wearing a crown?

Is this a frog or a Halloween kitten?

Is this a baby frog or Baby Fred?

Is this Santa Claus or Santa Frog?

Words to Know and Index

adults
pages 4, 19, 20, 21

bodies
pages 5, 6, 8, 16

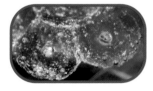

eggs
pages 4, 10, 11, 12, 13, 14, 20, 21

froglets
pages 18, 21

gills
pages 14, 16

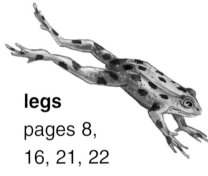

legs
pages 8, 16, 21, 22

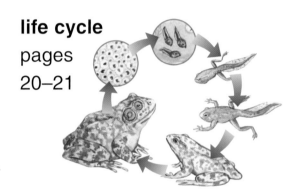

life cycle
pages 20–21

lungs
pages 8, 16

skin
pages 5, 6, 7, 8, 9, 22

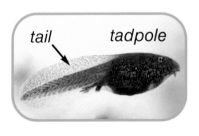

tadpoles
pages 11, 12, 13, 14, 15, 16, 17, 18, 21

tails
pages 8, 14, 18, 19, 21

Other index words
food pages 9, 18
hatching pages 14, 20, 21
metamorphosis page 10
senses page 9
toads page 22
toes pages 8, 19
tree frogs
pages 5, 8, 12, 13, 17, 18, 19

tree frog